G O D T H E O R Y
A Scientific Quest for God and The Cosmos

A Prequel to The Unified SuperStandard Model
A Composite, Functionally Triune God
The Necessity of an Everlasting, Divine Cosmos
Predestination vs. Free Will Resolved by Quantum Physics
God as Ultimate Quantum Observer-Witness
The Tape of Cosmic Existence
The Divine Cosmic Connection

Stephen Blaha Ph. D.
Blaha Research

Ex Scienta In Sapientia

Blaha

Pingree-Hill Publishing
MMXVIII

Cover: The cover displays the head of God from Michelangelo's ceiling in the Sistine Chapel at the Vatican.

Rev. 00/00/01   September 8, 2018

To My Grandchildren:

Nicholas, Milan, Maxim, and Alexandre

Some Other Books by Stephen Blaha

All the Megaverse! Starships Exploring the Endless Universes of the Cosmos using the Baryonic Force (Blaha Research, Auburn, NH, 2014)

SuperCivilizations: Civilizations as Superorganisms (McMann-Fisher Publishing, Auburn, NH, 2010)

All the Universe! Faster Than Light Tachyon Quark Starships & Particle Accelerators with the LHC as a Prototype Starship Drive Scientific Edition (Pingree-Hill Publishing, Auburn, NH, 2011).

The Unified SuperStandard Model and the Megaverse SECOND EDITION A Deeper Theory based on a New Particle Functional Space that Explicates Quantum Entanglement Spookiness (Pingree Hill Publishing, Auburn, NH, 2018).

Cosmos Creation: The Unified SuperStandard Model, Volume 2, SECOND EDITION (Pingree Hill Publishing, Auburn, NH, 2018).

Available on Amazon.com, bn.com Amazon.co.uk and other international web sites as well as at better bookstores (through Ingram Distributors).

CONTENTS

FIGURES and TABLES

INTRODUCTION

Most people on earth believe in a God of some form. In this book we will assume that God exists. We will address questions about God and the Cosmos (all of Creation) that can be answered by Logic and Scientific Analysis. We will see that surprising insights follow from this quest for knowledge of God and the Cosmos. A comparison of our findings with the descriptions of God and Creation in major religions shows a remarkable number of similarities. We leave it to the Readers to make of it what they will.

We were led to this study of God from a scientific view by the development of a fundamental Theory of Everything, The Unified SuperStandard Model, that we derived from a relatively simple set of axioms. (See Appendix A.) The set of axioms led to a derivation of The Unified SuperStandard Model that unifies all matter and their forces in a direct manner. The derivation is presented in volumes 1 and 2 of the Second Edition of *The Unified SuperStandard Model and the Megaverse*. It is not necessary to be familiar with these books except to realize these volumes provide a derivation of a Theory of Everything from basic axioms in the manner of Euclid's derivation of Geometry. Their beginning point was a "supposed" entity that follows certain "simple" rules to define the axioms governing the Cosmos and thereby leads to the derivation of the physical Cosmos. (The Cosmos consists of the entirety of Creation.)

A remarkable aspect of the "entity" is its similarity to features that most people attribute to God. This book makes a "leap of faith" and assumes It is God in Its physical aspects. We then take the universally agreed fundamental features of God and proceed to investigate the physical side of God's nature.

Some remarkable results follow: 1) God needs the Cosmos; 2) the Cosmos exists forever into the past and the future; 3) the Godhead consists of at least three parts: the Unmoved Mover, the Cosmos, and the Connection between them—functionally a triune God; 4)The Cosmos and Connection parts of God have a God-like spark that is present in the particles of the Unified SuperStandard Model (or perhaps a similar Theory of Everything); 5) Predestination and Free Will are made consistent by the Quantum nature of the Cosmos and the Connection.

The eternal natures of the Cosmos and the Connection have important implications for Physics. In particular, they may require an infinite chain of aeons of universes in which our universe is but one link in the chain. They are consistent with a Megaverse containing universes strewn through a higher dimensional space, much like galaxies are strewn throughout our universe.

1. Analyzing the Nature of God and the Cosmos

1.1 Reaching the Fundamental: God and Cosmos

This study of God[1] and the Cosmos is predicated on the belief that Physics, at the most fundamental level, can lead to a scientific view of God and the Cosmos.[2] This author developed a fundamental theory of Physics called The Unified SuperStandard Model[3] that derived Physics from a fundamental set of axioms in a manner analogous to Euclid's derivation of Geometry.

The basis of these axioms is an entity, called the Umoved Mover by many Philosophers and Theologians, who wished to "introduce" dynamical motions (change) in the Cosmos. The requirements for dynamics led to the axioms of the Unified SuperStandard Model.[4]

In turn, the nature of the Unmoved Mover became of interest as well as the general properties of the Cosmos. This book addresses these questions. Its approach to the dynamics of the Unmoved Mover does not

[1] **We assume that there is but one God - monotheism.** Some religions are *polytheistic* with many gods. However almost all polytheistic religions assume that one primary god exists that begins Creation and generates a family of secondary gods. In that sense polytheistic religions are "disguised" monotheistic religions.
[2] The Cosmos is all of Creation including matter and energy.
[3] See Blaha (2018a) which is based on a series of many books by the author starting in 1999.
[4] Blaha (2018b).

rely particularly on the Unified SuperStandard Model although that is where the questions originated. It can be viewed as based on any deep, fundamental Theory of Everything. The features of the Unmoved Mover presented in Blaha (2018b) are suggestive of what many view as God. However identifying the Unmoved Mover with God requires a leap of faith that many would make while others would not.

1.2 God in the Great Modern Religions

The Great, Modern Religions, Buddhism, Christianity, Confucianism, Hinduism, Islam, Judaism, Shintoism, Zoroastrianism, and so on, have varying views of God. Nevertheless, there is a great deal of commonality. Most of their descriptions of God are based on religious views, revelations, philosophic generalities, and other inspiration.

In this book we will approach God and the Cosmos based on logic and scientific concepts. We see this approach as solid and scientifically convincing although many aspects of God, described in religious writings, go much further into topics (such as emotions and morality) that a scientific approach cannot explain.

1.3 A Scientific Approach: Fundamental Tools

Assuming that God exists and is the Unmoved Mover of Philosophy and Theology (at least in part) we now describe the tools which, we believe, enable us to understand aspects of God and the

Cosmos, and to clarify conflicting concepts in the theologies of various religions.

1.3.1 Logic

The most important tool for the scientific understanding of any phenomena is Logic. We intend to apply Logic to the Divine, in a respectful way, to elucidate its features. (Some may remember that the consistency of Logic was questioned in the past based on apparent paradoxes and theorems such as Gödel's Theorem. In Blaha (2015a) we showed that these paradoxical results reflect a misunderstanding of the nature of logical statements. In particular, we pointed out that a statement is a form of function, stated in words and symbols, consisting of a predicate (the function) and a subject (the argument) that lies within the domain of the predicate (in the sense of function domains). Paradoxes and Gödel's Theorem use subjects (arguments) outside the domain of the predicates. In mathematics functions have allowed domains of arguments. So also do statements have allowed domains of subjects for their predicates.

Thus Logic is unblemished and can be applied without concern to any phenomena.

1.3.2 Scientific Tools of Space and Time

The scientific concepts that will form the basis of of the tools for understanding God and the Cosmos are space and time. We will not use complex details such as the Theory of Relativity but will merely use space and time, logically considered, to develop a partial understanding of God and the Cosmos.

1.3.3 Knowing Scientifically

By knowing of God and the Cosmos scientifically the Reader will see that many of the points of religious discussions and dissensions will be clarified and resolved.

2. God In Itself

The understanding of the nature of God in the World's Religions varies. There are many facets of God that Religions address. In this chapter we will examine the nature of God in Itself from a scientific view with *no* Cosmos present. God in Itself! Naturally the aspects of God that we will consider, within this context, are limited. We cannot, for example, scientifically consider God's emotions or other topics frequently discussed in religious literature. However we will find that our considerations are not without interest.

2.1 Unmoved Mover

If only God (the Unmoved Mover) exists, without any Cosmos or other things, then God has no physical nature, has no size or extension, and cannot change since time and space do not exist except as part of the Cosmos.

2.2 No Thought or Emotions

If God cannot change, then God would not be able to have any sequences of thought or emotion. Thus God would be an unchanging entity that could not, for example, create a Cosmos.

2.3 Loneliness

With only existence in itself, God only would be capable of permanent loneliness—not loneliness for any thing—but loneliness in itself.

2.4 What Do We Learn From These Considerations

Given the static nature of a God *alone*, God could not Create the Cosmos at some specific instant. For that would violate the above found constraints despite the assumption of a God with unlimited power and abilities.

2.5 The Cosmos has No Beginning and No End

We conclude that the Cosmos must always have been in existence. A lonely God with nothing else "present" cannot have ever existed. For then there would be no Creation of the Cosmos.

3. The Cosmos in Itself

3.1 What is the Cosmos?

We define the Cosmos to be all of Creation including all matter and energy in galaxies, our universe and any other universes that might exist. (We called the space of all universes the Megaverse in earlier books.) Since the Cosmos has dynamical evolution, time must be defined in all universes and the Megaverse (if it exists). And space must exist within, and between, universes for dynamics to take place. Perhaps the best way to view the Megaverse is by analogy with our universe. The Megaverse is analogous to our universe with its universes analogous to galaxies and the space between its universes analogous to the space between galaxies.

3.1.1 Reasons for Believing in Other Universes

In Blaha (2018a) we gave a number of experimental reasons based on astrophysical concepts that we reproduce here for the reader's convenience:

At first glance it would seem impossible to produce evidence for the existence of other universes. However there are subtle means by which we can 'sense' experimentally 'nearby' universes should they exist. The mechanism would appear to be gravitational effects exerted on objects within our universe by unseen objects of enormous mass. Currently there appears to be three experimental suggestions of the existence of 'nearby' universes and one theoretical argument based on an influx of mass-energy from the Megaverse that may support an understanding of the expansion of our universe.

30.2.1 Great Attractors

One potential support is the discovery of the Great Attractor (at the center of the Laniakea Galaxy Supercluster), and the more massive Shapley Attractor (centered in the Shapley Supercluster)[5]. These attractors contain massive numbers of galaxies and are drawing galaxies over a distance of millions of light years towards them.

If another universe(s) is 'near' our universe it could act as a 'gravitational magnet' and draw galaxies within our universe towards it to form one or more superclusters which could then act as attractors. Thus attractors might indirectly reveal the presence of other nearby universes—contrary to the expected large scale uniformity of the universe. The only other apparent source of superclusters is chance. Chance seems an unsatisfactory possibility in the present case.

30.2.2 Bright Bumps in Universe Sugesting Collision with Another Universe

A recent study[6] of the residual brightness of parts of the accessible universe found that bright patches appeared if a model of the CMB (Cosmic Microwave Background) with gases, stars and dust was 'subtracted' from the PLANCK map of the entire sky. After the subtraction one would expect only noise spread throughout the sky. However, bright patches were seen in a certain range of frequencies. These anomalies are thought to be a result of our universe colliding with another object – presumably another universe in the Megaverse.

---

[5] Tully, R. Brent; Courtois, Helene; Hoffman, Yehuda; Pomarède, Daniel, "The Laniakea Supercluster of galaxies". Nature (4 September 2014). 513 (7516): 71–73; arXiv:1409.0880.
[6] Ranga-Ram Chary, arXiv.org:/1510.00126 (2015).

30.2.3 Cold Spot in Universe Suggesting Collision with Another Universe

Another recent study[7] of a huge cold region of the universe spanning billions of light years revealed that this region is not a relatively empty region but rather is similar to in its distribution of galaxies to the rest of the universe. Previous the Cold Spot (an area where cosmic microwave background radiation – the leftover Big Bang radiation is weak – making it significantly colder (0.00015C colder) than the average temperature of the universe.)

An analysis of 7,000 galaxy redshifts using new high-resolution data has now shown that the Cold Spot is similar to the rest of the universe. The Durham University group suggested that the Cold Spot might have been caused by a collision between our universe and another Universe. They further suggested that there is only a 1 in 50 chance that it could explained by standard cosmology. could produce this feature

Thus we have another important piece of circumstantial evidence in favor of other universes and thus the Megaverse.

30.2.4 Megaverse Energy-Matter Infusion into Our Universe

In chapter 14 of Blaha (2017c) we presented a model for an influx of mass-energy from the Megaverse to support the Bondi-Gold-Hoyle-Narlikar Steady State Cosmology, which was originally based on the 'continuous creation of mass-energy' by Hoyle and Narliker. This model explains why the value of Ω makes the universe close to flat. If this model is correct then we would have concrete support for a Megaverse with a low mass-energy density leaking mass-energy into our universe. *More generally, it suggests that universes are surfaces of high mass-energy density in a Megaverse of low mass-energy density – with a ratio of mass-energy densities of the other of 10^{30}.*

30.2.5 Conclusion

We conclude that data is beginning to emerge favoring multiple universes and a physical Megaverse in support of the theoretical justifications presented earlier.

---

[7] T. Shanks et al, Durham University (Australia), Monthly Notices of the Royal Astronomical Society, 2016 .

There are also important theoretical arguments for believing in the Megaverse. See Blaha (2018a).

3.1.2 The Cosmos and Possible Non-Physical Additional Spaces: Heaven, Hell and So On

The physical Cosmos is briefly described above. A number of Religions suggest that other "spaces" of a non-physical nature exist such as Heaven, Hell, and so on. The consideration of these "spaces" is beyond the scope of Physics and so will not be considered in this book.

3.2 How Did It Start or Did It Always Exist?

In the previous chapter we showed that the Cosmos must always have existed due to the nature of God. This conclusion leads to the following possibilities:

1. If the Cosmos consists only of our universe then our universe must have existed into the infinite past. The universe may have been subject to oscillations in size from a point (a Big Bang point) to some large size. Or it may have been a point for an infinite amount of time and then "one day" it began expansion. Both possibilities have been considered by theoretical physicists.[8]

---

[8] Another possibility that has surfaced recently is that our universe is but one of an infinite succession of universes that persist from aeon to aeon. A signature of this succession of universes would be Hawking points that are shadowy remnants of past universes. See D. An, K. A.

2. If the Cosmos is a Megaverse with any number (innumerable?) of universes within it, then universes can interact (collide), generate new universes, destroy universes, and so on. Then our universe may be one universe that came into existence at some remote time and persists.

In any case the Cosmos must have existed forever and will continue to exist forever into the future. The reason is simple: If the Cosmos should begin or end at some time then God would be in a static state before or after as described in chapter 2. If this happened we would have a God that is time-dependent contrary to our assumption of a God who exists independent of time. Time is, after all, an artifact (part) of the Cosmos and does not exist independent of the Cosmos.
The Cosmos has always existed and will exist forever.

3.3 How May God View the Cosmos?

In view of eternal nature of the Cosmos, we may rightly inquire of God's view of the Cosmos. Perhaps the best view that God might have of the Cosmos is that of an infinite tape recording everything in the

---

Meissner, R. Penrose, "Apparent Evidence for Hawking Points in the CMB Sky" arXiv:1808.01740 (2018) for a theoretical discussion. Suggestive new evidence from the BICEP 2 team for Hawking points is presented in D. An, K. A. Meissner, and P. Nurowski, Mon. Not. Roy. Astron. Soc 3251, **473** (2018).

Cosmos in infinite detail. God views the tape in its entirety always since he must know all. God does not need time travel since He/She exists with perfect knowledge of eternity always.

3.4 Predestination

Given God's perfect knowledge of the past and future, one might think that *Predestination* follows. Predestination "removes" free will by making all events predetermined by the "inexorable will of God." A person does not have freedom of choice (free will) in this view but consciously or unconsciously follows God's will.

In chapter 7 we will consider Predestination and will show that God knows the past, present and future completely, and yet free will (choice) still exists in the Cosmos if the Cosmos is Quantum.

3.5 The Limitless Power of God Over the Cosmos

The limitless power of God is a true fact[9] but since the infinite past and future is fully known to God, God's power is seen, by God, to have been exercised at specific points in the Cosmos' evolution.

God sees the Cosmos "tape" in its entirety, so all God's "acts" are known to God for "all time."

---

[9] By our initial assumption of a limitless God.

4. Physical Aspects of the "Creation" of the Cosmos

4.1 Was the Cosmos Created?

In chapters 2 and 3 we saw that the Cosmos must always have existed and must continue to exist forever. In this chapter we examine why the Cosmos has the form that it has by considering the fictitious case of an initial creation of the Cosmos. We ask why[10] did God create the Cosmos in the manner in which he did?

4.2 God's Apparent Creation Rationale

The derivation of the Physical theory[11] of the Cosmos, as we know it, has certain fundamental prerequisites if one wishes to have dynamical physical processes, as we know them, to occur. Any attempt to create a universal physical theory must meet these prerequsites.

---

[10] The Creation of the Cosmos was considered in Blaha (2018b).
[11] Blaha (2018a) and (2018b) present a complete "Theory of Everything" for the Cosmos. The reader does not need to know the details of the theory to understand this chapter and following chapters.

4.3 Some Fundamental Prerequisites for a Fundamental Physics Theory of the Cosmos

We can list some[12] fundamental prerequisites based on a general knowledge of the necessary nature of a fundamental theory of Physics.

1) A time variable must exist that may have various forms,

2) We wish to have a dynamical fundamental theory that evolves in time. Thus there must be a mechanism(s) that allow dynamical processes to exist that may, or may not, run in parallel.

3) Multiple parallel processes can execute.

4) There must be a space with a coordinate system(s), and a distance measure, within which processes can execute.

5) There must be wave-particles upon which dynamical processes execute.

6) The theory must be Quantum.

7) Creation should opt for Vitamorphic[13] universes that support life in some form. Recent studies have shown that evolution

---

[12] Blaha (2018b) contains a more complete list.

[13] The *Vitamorphic Principle* states that universes should support some form of life realizing that there are many varieties of life and borderline forms of life. A 'tight' definition of life has not been satisfactorily constructed. There are many borderline entities that may or may not be called life. We take 'Vitamorphic' to mean 'life enabling' in English. Vitamorphism is not a concept without meaning—a universe (Megaverse) consisting of only inert matter without energy present

favors the development of increasingly intelligent life. Thus the ultimate appearance of intelligent life at places within universes appears to be natural, making the *Anthropic Principle* an evolutionary consequence[14] of the *Vitamorphic Principle*.

These prerequisites would seem to be necessary and "sufficient" for the specification of a fundamental Physics theory of the Cosmos.

---

would be non-Vitamorphic. The Anthropic Principle, briefly put, states that intelligent human-like life should exist. We pronounce "Vitamorphic" in Latin style as "Veeta-morphic."

[14] One can well wonder whether the emergence and dominance of Mankind has eliminated the possibility of the emergence of other intelligent species on earth from the many semi-intelligent species that exist now and in the past.

5. God's Composite Nature

5.1 God and the Cosmos

In earlier chapters we saw that God (the Unmoved Mover) requires the Cosmos to have a dynamic aspect. The Unmoved Mover specifies the nature of the Cosmos through the considerations of chapter 4 which lead to the axioms presented in Appendix A. The derivation of The Theory of Everything in Blaha (2018a) and (2018b) gives the Standard Model of Elementary Particles plus much more. The Unmoved Mover causes the dynamics (the "Movement") of the evolving Cosmos. As we saw earlier the Cosmos exists forever so the Creation of the Cosmos by the Unmoved Mover, although it is done by God, is "before time" since time is an artifact of the Cosmos and did not exist before Creation. Thus Creation does not happen at some instant but really exists forever as an "implicit" part of God (the Unmoved Mover).

5.2 Is the Cosmos Part of God?

Or does God permeate the Cosmos? If the Cosmos is a distinct part of a Godhead composed of the Unmoved Mover, the Cosmos, and perhaps additional parts then we must ask how does the Cosmos partake of God-like features. If we regard the Cosmos as merely matter and energy, as Physicists view it, then there is no Godliness in the Cosmos. So only an enhanced theory of the Cosmos would be required such as that of Leibniz[15] where particles of matter and energy have a divine "spark." An enhanced theory of the Cosmos would put the Cosmos on a God-like footing and unite It with the Unmoved Mover. See Table 5.1 for a comparison of features of God and the Cosmos. The fact that they both exist forever is a strong argument for a God-like Cosmos. Spinoza suggested a similar pantheistic view of the Cosmos. Karl Krause coined a name for a version of this view, which he called *panentheism*.

A panentheistic view of the Cosmos distinguishes the Cosmos from the Unmoved Mover. So we must consider the possibility that the Godhead has at least two parts: the Unmoved Mover and the "panentheistic" Cosmos that acquires "Godhood" in Its particles of matter and energy—perhaps through divine sparks (monads?) or a similar mechanism.

The godliness of the Godhead then is due to the godliness of Its parts—a primary feature of godliness is its infinity of existence.

5.3 God's Relation to the Cosmos – The Connection

We have distinguished the Unmoved Mover from the Cosmos with both partaking of the Godhead. The Unmoved Mover is connected to the Cosmos by causing natural laws to be obeyed throughout the

---

[15] Leibniz viewed all particles of matter as containing a devine spark – his *monad* theory. See Rescher (1967).

Cosmos. It is also possible that the Unmoved Mover, by exerting Its will and unlimited power, may cause events (interventions) to take place within the Cosmos that we might view as miracles or at least strange phenomena. (Chapter 7 describes a mechanism for God to act in the Cosmos to achieve Its will without violating the Physical laws of the Unified SuperStandard Model.)

The *Connection* between the Unmoved Mover and the Cosmos could be viewed as simply a "transmission" between them. It might also be viewed as an entity with properties that may be "God-like." From previous chapters we see the Connection must be eternal—without beginning or end. The nature of the Connection must partake of the divinity of the Unmoved Mover and the Cosmos to achieve dynamical control of the Cosmos by the Unmoved Mover, and to support intervention by the Unmoved Mover in the Cosmos. The method by which it achieves these goals is in the interaction between the Unmoved Mover and the Cosmos.

If the Cosmos has a spark of divinity, then the Connection—connecting both divine parts—must have a divine aspect: its "infinitesimal" parts must also have a spark of the divine.[16]

Thus we arrive at *a triune Godhead consisting of the Unmoved Mover, the Cosmos, and the Connection between them.* Table 5.1

---

[16] Perhaps as Leibniz-like monads. See chapter 6 for a "particulate" form of Connection.

compares the features of the parts.[17] Fig. 5.1 diagrams the interrelations of the parts in the Godhead.

Is there one God? Yes, according to our assumption and ensuing discussion. We merely provide a logical separation of God into parts.

In chapter 6 we will discuss the nature of the Connection in some detail within the framework of our Unified SuperStandard Model. Lay readers may choose to skip this somewhat technical chapter since it does not play a role in the discussions in succeeding chapters.

ENTITY	NATURE	LIFETIME	ROLE
Unmoved Mover	Spirit	Forever	Creates and Causes Dynamics
Cosmos	Spirit/Material	Forever	Scene of dynamic Activity

---

[17] One cannot say that the three parts of the Godhead are as separated as our analytical discussion suggests. They may well be inseparable. Also, the possibility of other parts is not precluded.

Connection	Spirit	Forever	Connects God, as Unmoved Mover, to the Cosmos, and intervenes in Cosmos events

Table 5.1. The entities of existence. The Cosmos can be viewed as spirit if all forces between its parts are zero. In reality there are forces and so the Cosmos is "material.".

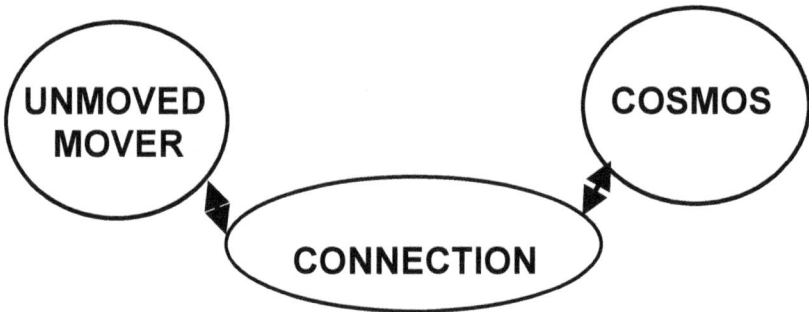

Figure 5.1. Relations between the three logical parts of the Godhead. The lines between the parts signify the "communications" channels between the parts..

6. Possible Mechanism for the Connection Part of God

This chapter describes a possible mechanism for the Connection based on our Unified SuperStandard Model.[18]

The "union" of the Connection with the Cosmos is implemented by associating *two* quantum fields with every particle of matter and energy.[19] In Blaha (2018a) and (2018b) we implemented this formulation of the SuperStandard Model for major technical reasons summarized below in section 6.1.

Based on our preceding discussions here, we now attribute a greater significance to the two field formulation. We identify one of the fields, in each pair of fields for a particle, as a Connection field that supports the roles of the Connection: 1) as forcing reality to conform to the Laws of Physics as set up by the Unmoved Mover, and 2) as implementing possible "Divine Intervention" by the Unmoved Mover. This field is typically labeled with a "1". The other field, which we label with the index "2", is a Cosmos field that generates the physical

---

[18] Much of the material appeared in Blaha (2018a) and (2018b).
[19] Both boson and fermion particles.

dynamics of Reality manipulating matter and energy. The dynamics equations are the result of the Connection fields in a lagrangian formulation.

In this book we have assumed that all particles of matter and energy have a spark of divinity within them that taken together makes both the Cosmos and Connection divine. Thus the fields of both type "1" and type "2" have a divine spark within them (when their particle relation is considered) by assumption—an assumption required in order to have a divine Cosmos and a divine Connection.

6.1 Technical Reasons for "Two Fields per Particle" Formulation

The Unified SuperStandard Model, and earlier work, pioneered the use of a quantum field theoretic formalism that associated two second quantized fields with every elementary particle. The two field formalism was also used to develop a generalization of Quantum Mechanics that united classical fields with quantum fields. (This formalism enabled a "continuous" transformation (rotation) to be made between strictly quantum fields and "corresponding" strictly classical fields.

In the Unified SuperStandard Model we used the two second quantized fields formalism in four situations:

1. The formalism was applied to Higgs boson fields to obtain a formulation that cleanly separated the vacuum expectation value of a Higgs particle's field from its second quantized part.

2. The formalism was applied to higher derivative dynamic parts to obtain a canonical lagrangian formulation via the Ostrogradski Bootstrap mechanism. The higher derivative sector generated quark confinement through a manifest linear potential, and a gravitational potential that had three forms depending on distance in a manner similar to MOND gravity. But without modifying fundamental Newtonian law.

3. The formalism resolves the well-known problem of ambiguities between second quantization in different reference frames. In the 1970's the author showed that the formalism could resolve second quantization ambiguities using Bogoliubov transformations. Second quantization then becomes "covariant" under changes of coordinate systems.

4. The two field formalism, if used in Quantum Mechanics, supports continuous transformations between quantum mechanics and classical mechanics, and allows for pseudo-quantum mechanics intermediate between quantum mechanics and classical mechanics. Such intermediate mechanics may appear in the "gray" zone that one sometimes sees in atomic theory.

6.2 Divine Cosmos and Divine Connection

The Connection is god-like through sparks of godliness within the fields of type "1" that are like the *qubes* and *qubas* of matter and energy in the universe (and the Megaverse) in our Unified SuperStandard Model.

The Unified SuperStandard Model specifies the dynamics of the divine Cosmos through the control on type "2" fields exerted by the type "1" fields of the Connection. Both Connection and Cosmos have Qubes and Qubas containing divine sparks.

The Unmoved Mover uses the Connection to constrain the Cosmos to obey Physical Laws and to possibly intervene in the Cosmos.

7. Predestination, Free Will and Quantum Theory

Fixed Fate, free will, foreknowledge absolute.
J. Milton, *Paradise Lost*, Book ii, line 560

Predestination is a troubling concept that is accepted in some religions and rejected by others. It states that all events happen through the design of God and that free will does not truly exist—it is an illusion.

In this chapter we will suggest that Quantum Theory enables free will to exist, enables God to intervene in the Cosmos, and yet enables God to be all-knowing of events past and future in all detail with "foreknowledge absolute.".

7.1 God's Tape of the Cosmos and Predestination

Earlier we suggested the view that God, in effect, has an infinite tape containing all aspects of the Cosmos from the remote past to the remote future. His foreknowledge indicates that he is fully aware of the entire contents of the tape everlastingly in the past and future.

God's "foreknowledge absolute" is the predestination to which many religions refer. It appears to eliminate the possibility of arbitrary intervention by God into Cosmic events at selected points in a manner not present in the tape. Yet any intervention must appear in the tape since it is a faithful record of eternity.

Thus God cannot arbitrarily and randomly intervene in Cosmic events—superficially contradicting God's assumed limitless power. However, a moment's thought shows that all interventions at various times in the "life" of the Cosmos must have existed as a reality forever—from the infinite past—with its consequences for the infinite future of the Cosmos. The tape contains all interventions at all times.

7.2 The Need for a Quantum Cosmos

In Blaha (2018a) we suggested that Quantum Theory was the simplest way to ensure that matter and energy were both made of discrete particles.

We now consider another, perhaps deeper, justification for Quantum Theory. While Quantum Theory has many facets, one fact of great importance in our view, is that it introduces chance into physical processes. When an event takes place, such as the collision of two particles, there can be varying results of the collision. Each possible result has a certain probability of happening—just as flipping a coin has a probability of "coming up" heads and a probability of "coming up" tails.

7.2.1 God's Intervention in the Cosmos

The introduction of chance in physical events opens a "new" possibility for God's intervention in Cosmic events. Without chance God's intervention would have to be strictly limited by Physical Law (which He established absolutely) making "miracles" very limited, and in most cases impossible.

With chance in physical events it becomes possible for God to "tweak" an event making a certain result happen. This result can then cause further events to happen, followed by yet further events, and so on.

The result is a cascading set of events caused by an initial tweak consistent with quantum probability—a chain reaction of events that can generate a miracle or even change history. One remembers here the lament of Richard III of England, "My kingdom for a horse." (We will not comment on the chain of events that would have put a horse within Richard's grasp.)

7.2.2 Quantum Source of Free Will

Free will is usually viewed from the aspect of a complete individual in terms of the person's mental state. However, free will has several forms. Some forms relate to the person's perceived situation with free will exercised to maximize the person's benefit and/or views. This form involves a significant part of the person's consciousness.

Another form of free will is chance decisions. A good example of this form is spot decisions as to where to place chips on a roulette table.

This type of decision can be based on guessing and may reflect a chance event in a person's mind. Free will based on chance miniscule events in a person's mind can be the result of cascading quantum chance.

Thus a person has free will without God's intervention. But God can also intervene by making a quantum choice of outcome in a person's neurons.

God can thus intervene in the Cosmos to implement change, guide free will, and execute miracles through Quantum effects.

7.3 Quantum Observer Problem

Having brought in Quantum Theory to support intervention by God we must now consider an important Quantum Theory problem that is resolved by the existence of God.

The problem is the need for a Quantum Observer to view an event and observe which of the possible results actually occurs in reality. A famous example is Schrödinger's Cat. A cat is placed in a box with a radioactive element that decays after a "random" time. The setup in the box causes the cat to die when the radioactive element decays. The problem is: After x minutes is the cat alive or dead? The answer can only be found if the box is opened by an observer. Before that point in time the cat is in an unknown state with the reality of its life in doubt.

Thus reality becomes an issue of observation. Some have suggested that complete knowledge of the entire element-cat-box apparatus as a quantum state would resolve the issue. But that is unlikely because the composite system is quantum and subject to chance as well.

One could extend the apparatus state to the entire universe. But that would still be quantum.

So the tenure of the cat's lifetime remains uncertain forever. A sad situation.

The situation of Schrödinger's Cat applies throughout the Cosmos. It appears that reality is an everpresent issue for the Cosmos.

7.4 God as the Ultimate Quantum Observer

The only clear-cut solution to the reality problem is God—the Ultimate Quantum Observer. God need only look at His "tape" to see the results of all Quantum events. Thus God gives reality to the Cosmos.

7.5 Events Without Observers

The question raised in some religions: does an acorn make a sound when it falls to the ground if no one is present to hear the sound, is resolved. God, the Unmoved Mover, is the omniscient Observer in all quantum and non-quantum events. It makes reality real whether or not a human observer is present.

8. God Theory Results

8.1 God's Nature from a Scientific Perspective

This work began by extending the possibility raised by the Unified SuperStandard Model in Blaha (2018b) that the entity we previously called the Unmoved Mover was in fact God. Then with that assumption, and the presumed features of the Godhead, we proceeded to apply Physical thought and Logic to obtain a theory of God's nature from a scientific perspective.

We did not consider aspects of God that dominate theological discussions: Its mercy, Its Love, Its relation to Good and Evil, and so on. These topics do not appear to be susceptible to Scientific analysis.

Nevertheless we obtained a view of God with noteworthy features that is consistent with much theological thought in most major religions. Our findings support notions of God that are prevalent in many religions. But they have a solid sciuentific/logical basis. Theological discussions are often based on principles that are founded in religious belief. A scientific basis with the primary assumption of one God and the secondary reality of the existence of the Cosmos has the ring of a deeper, more convincing Truth.

8.2 A Scientific View of God

Our major findings are:

1) The part of God called the Unmoved Mover needs the Cosmos.

2) The Cosmos exists forever in the past and the future. It is divine just as the Unmoved Mover.

3) The Unmoved Mover and the Cosmos are 'joined" by a part called the Connection which exists forever and is divine as well.

4) The Connection implements the dynamics of Physical Laws in the Cosmos and performs any intervention required by the Unmoved Mover.

5) The Godhead consists of at least three divine parts: the Unmoved Mover, the Cosmos, and the Connection between them. Together the parts functionally form a triune God.

6) The Cosmos and Connection parts of God have a God-like nature that is represented in the Cosmos within the dynamics of the Unified SuperStandard Model or a similar Theory of Everything.

7) The Godliness present in the Cosmos, and the Connection, resides in a divine "spark" within the particles[20] of matter and energy within them—a form of panentheism.

8) The apparent contradiction between Predestination and Free Will is resolved by Quantum Theory.

8.3 Conclusion

We have developed a scientific analysis of God that joins naturally with our physical theory: The Unified SuperStandard Model. As a result we have a chain of logic from an ultimate being, a divine Euclid, to a derivation of the form of Physical Reality as we know it, and additional features that remain to be found experimentally.

The similarity of our conclusions with the general form of modern major religions is encouraging.

---

[20] The divine spark resides within the Qubes and Qubas in particles and energy in our Unified SuperStandard Model.

Appendix A. Enhanced Form of Unified SuperStandard Model Axioms

For the Reader's convenience we reproduce chapter 3 of Blaha (2018b) in this Appendix.

A.1 Underlying Basis of SuperStandard Axioms

In this chapter we present a revised set[21] of 'primitive' terms and axioms for our theory. A comparison of this new set of axioms with those provided in the Book will show that they are equivalent but add a few new axioms. They are also more simply stated, have fewer overlaps between axions, and cleanly lead to the Book's theory of elementary particles.

The goal of the Book and this volume is to derive the Unified SuperStandard Model in the manner of Euclid with a clear connection between the steps of the derivation just as Euclid developed geometry from a progression of theorems.

---

[21] The Book is Blaha (2018b). The Book presents axioms in chapter 0.

A.2 Primitive Terms and Axioms

Primitive terms can be as simple as those of Euclid or they can be more complex. The level of simplicity depends on the nature of the theory and the Physical Laws that emerge from it. In the case at hand, a fundamental unified theory, the constructs that emerge in the construction of the theory are mathematically complex. Consequently, the choice of primitive terms and axioms may be expected to be mathematically complex as well, unless one wishes to expand the primitive terms into a more detailed, term by term description in simpler, more basic primitives. We will not pursue that alternative here since the terms that we use are 'self-explanatory' to the Elementary Particle Physics theorist knowledgable about quantum field theory and particle symmetries.

A.3 Mathematics and Conceptual Prerequisites

Due to the complexity of the Theory we have chosen to specify mathematics prerequisites and use them in the derivation rather than devoting parts of the derivation to mathematical preliminaries. Therefore we use complex variable theory, Riemannian coordinates, group theory, classical and Quantum Logic, functionals, Chomsky-like computational languages, and so on without bringing in unnecessary supporting details from them.

We also assume certain physical concepts such as distance, quantum features, second quantization, covariance under a group transformation, and spatial curvature.

The list of axioms uses some of these prerequisite concepts treating them as primitive terms for the derivation.

A.4 Primitive Terms for the Unified SuperStandard Model

The somewhat revised set of primitive terms of the theory are:

Qubits
Qubes
Qubas
Core
Grammar
Terminal and Nonterminal Symbols
Production Rules
Speed of Light
Spatial Dimensions
Space and Time Coordinates
Covariance under group transformations
Asynchronous processes
Parallel Processes
Reference Frame
Complex Lorentz Group
General Coordinate Transformations
Gravity
Universe
Particle Masses

Fermions
Bosons
Particle States
Particle Rest State
Particle Momenta
Spin
Canonical Quantization
Quantum Process
Quantum Entanglement
Second Quantization
Quantum Field Theory
Quantum States
Asymptotic Particle States
Internal Symmetries
Coupling Constants
Discrete Symmetries
Yang-Mills Local Gauge Theory
Functionals
Functional space

In choosing these primitives, we understand that they generally embody a significant theoretic description or body of knowledge. We do not include names used in the mapping to reality (such as quark) in the list of primitives since the mapping to reality is a separate issue in our view.

A.5 Revised Axiom Set for the Unified SuperStandard Model

The somewhat revised set of axioms that we list below is supplemented by the Decision Axioms of Appendix C.1.3 of the Book. The 'new' physical axioms are

PARTICLE AXIOMS

1. All matter and energy is composed of particles.
2. Each fundamental particle has a physico-logic structure within it that we designate its core.
3. Particles form an alphabet with a finite number of characters and combine in ways specified by the quantum probabilistic production rules of a quantum computational grammar.[22]
4. A core is a particle functional that combines with a free field fourier coordinate expansion in an inner product to produce a free second quantized particle field.
5. There is a 4-dimensional space of particle functionals, called *particle functional space*,with the distance measure eq. A.1 specifying the transformation group of particle functionals.
6. Particle functional space consists of a single point.
7. The core of a fermion functional is called a *qube*. Fundamental bosons have a core consisting of a boson functional called a *quba*.
8. Qubes have a a bare mass. Qubas have zero mass.

SPACE AXIOMS

---

[22] See Blaha (2005b).

9. The dimensions of a coordinate space-time are determined by the number of fundamental[23] interactions, and the requirement that all parallel processes, with parts perhaps separated by distances, can occur synchronously.
10. Spatial coordinates are inherently complex-valued.
11. Space has one complex-valued component that plays the role of time. Physical phenomena dynamically evolve based on the time variable.
12. The infinitesimal distance ds between two space-time points is given by

$$ds^2 = dt^2 - d\mathbf{x}^2 \qquad\qquad (A.1)$$

where $d\mathbf{x}$ is a vector of the spatial coordinates. Transformations between coordinate systems preserve the value of ds and define a transformation group. (The Complex Lorentz Group)

13. Physically acceptable reference frames have real-valued coordinates. These coordinates can be obtained by group transformations from complex-valued coordinate systems. Physical space-time measurements are made in a real-valued coordinate system.
14. The speed of light is the same in all reference frames.
15. Free fundamental leptons must have a real-valued energy.
16. Gravity may cause space-time to be curved. (Complex General Coordinate transformations[24])

---

[23] Interactions that would exist in the absence of fermion particles.

[24] If the metric tensor of space-time is analogous to one of the metric tensors of the superfluid phases of ^{3}He, then space-time might have several metric tensors in 'various regions.' If the space-time metric tensor is analogous to the ^{3}He-B superfluid phase metric tensor, which has an effective gravity with a complex metric tensor, the space-time metric tensor would be the familiar one of General Relativity. However if the space-time metric tensor is analogous to the metric tensor of superfluid ^{3}He-A, which exists at higher pressure and temperature, then the space-time metric tensor might be similar to the Penrose twistor theory metric tensor. In this case the

DYNAMICS AXIOMS

17. The complete theory has a lagrangian formulation. If the lagrangian is truncated to quadratic form (interactions set to zero) then symmetries appear that are the source of particle symmeytry groups that persist with broken symmetry after interactions are reintroduced. The lagrangian specifies a set of production rules of a type 0 Chomsky language generalized to include production rules for the generation of all strings of symbols (particles) from any strings of symbols (including the *head symbol*.)[25]
18. The lagrangian of the theory must be invariant under coordinate system transformations.
19. Dynamical particle equations must be covariant under group transformations.
20. All interactions have a local Yang-Mills gauge theory formulation.
21. The vector bosons, and the interactions among them, are determined by terms in complete lagrangian, some of whose parts are obtained from the Riemann-Christoffel Curvature Tensor.

QUANTIZATION AXIOMS

22. All fields must be canonically quantized.
23. Fermion and Boson vacua can be defined that are valid in all coordinate systems.
24. The number of particles in an asymptotic state of any given type is invariant in all reference frames.
25. Quantum processes starting in an initial quantum state, with parts separated by a distance after a time, can have the parts synchronously change each other instantaneously. (Quantum Entanglement)

---

corresponding General Relativity may have a twistor-like metric tensor: perhaps in the early universe, and/or inside black holes, and/or in small universes with higher pressure and temperature than our universe. We will assume the conventional metric for Complex Special and General Relativity.

[25] Chapter 8 of Blaha (2018b) discusses computational languages for particles in detail.

REFERENCES

Blaha, S., 1998, *Cosmos and Consciousness 2ndEdition* (Pingree-Hill Publishing, Auburn, NH, 2003).

_____, 2014c, *All the Megaverse! II Between Megaverse Universes: Quantum Entanglement Explained by the Megaverse Coherent Baryonic Radiation Devices – PHASERs Neutron Star Megaverse Slingshot Dynamics Spiritual and UFO Events, and the Megaverse Microscopic Entry into the Megaverse* (Blaha Research, Auburn, NH, 2014).

_____, 2015a, *PHYSICS IS LOGIC PAINTED ON THE VOID: Origin of Bare Masses and The Standard Model in Logic, U(4) Origin of the Generations, Normal and Dark Baryonic Forces, Dark Matter, Dark Energy, The Big Bang, Complex General Relativity, A Megaverse of Universe Particles* (Blaha Research, Auburn, NH, 2015).

_____, 2015b, *PHYSICS IS LOGIC Part II: The Theory of Everything, The Megaverse Theory of Everything, U(4)⊗U(4) Grand Unified Theory (GUT), Inertial Mass = Gravitational Mass, Unified Extended Standard Model and a New Complex General Relativity with Higgs Particles, Generation Group Higgs Particles* (Blaha Research, Auburn, NH, 2015).

_____, 2016e, *MoND: Unification of the Strong Interactions and Gravitation II, Quark Confinement Linked to Large-Scale Gravity, Physics is Logic IX* (Blaha Research, Auburn, NH, 2016).

_____, 2016f, *CQ Mechanics: A Unification of Quantum & Classical Mechanics, Quantum/Semi-Classical Entanglement, Quantum/Classical Path Integrals, Quantum/Classical Chaos* (Blaha Research, Auburn, NH, 2016).

_____, 2016g, *GEMS: Unified Gravity, ElectroMagnetic and Strong Interactions: Manifest Quark Confinement, A Solution for the Proton Spin Puzzle, Modified Gravity on the Galactic Scale* (Pingree Hill Publishing, Auburn, NH, 2016).

_____, 2016h, *Unification of the Seven Boson Interactions based on the Riemann-Christoffel Curvature Tensor* (Pingree Hill Publishing, Auburn, NH, 2016).

_____, 2017c, *Megaverse: The Universe of Universes* (Pingree Hill Publishing, Auburn, NH, 2017).
_____, 2017f, *The Unified SuperStandard Model in Our Universe and the Megaverse: Quarks, ... ,* (Pingree Hill Publishing, Auburn, NH, 2017).

_____, 2018a, *The Unified SuperStandard Model and the Megaverse SECOND EDITION A Deeper Theory based on a New Particle Functional Space that Explicates Quantum Entanglement Spookiness (Volume 1)* (Pingree Hill Publishing, Auburn, NH, 2018).

_____, 2018b, *Cosmos Creation: The Unified SuperStandard Model, Volume 2, SECOND EDITION* (Pingree Hill Publishing, Auburn, NH, 2018).

Rescher, N., 1967, *The Philosophy of Leibniz* (Prentice-Hall, Englewood Cliffs, NJ, 1967).

INDEX

About the Author

Stephen Blaha is a well known Physicist and Man of Letters with interests in Science, Society and civilization, the Arts, and Technology. He had an Alfred P. Sloan Foundation scholarship in college. He received his Ph.D. in Physics from Rockefeller University. He has served on the faculties of several major universities. He was also a Member of the Technical Staff at Bell Laboratories, a manager at the Boston Globe Newspaper, a Director at Wang Laboratories, and President of Blaha Software Inc and of Janus Associates Inc. (NH).

Among other achievements he was a co-discoverer of the "r potential" for heavy quark binding developing the first (and still the only demonstrable) non-abelian gauge theory with an "r" potential; first suggested the existence of topological structures in superfluid He-3; first proposed Yang-Mills theories would appear in condensed matter phenomena with non-scalar order parameters; first developed a grammar-based formalism for quantum computers and applied it to elementary particle theories; first developed a new form of quantum field theory without divergences (thus solving a major 60 year old problem that enabled a unified theory of the Standard Model and Quantum Gravity without divergences to be developed); first developed a formulation of complex General Relativity based on analytic continuation from real space-time; first developed a generalized non-homogeneous Robertson-Walker metric that enabled a quantum theory of the Big Bang to be developed without singularities at t = 0; first generalized Cauchy's theorem and Gauss' theorem to complex, curved multi-dimensional spaces; received Honorable Mention in the Gravity Research Foundation Essay Competition in 1978; first developed a physically acceptable theory of faster-than-light particles; first derived a composition of extrema method in the Calculus of Variations; first quantitatively suggested that inflationary periods in the history of the universe were not needed; first proved Gödel's Theorem implies Nature must be quantum; provided a new alternative to the Higgs Mechanism, and Higgs particles, to generate masses; first showed how to resolve logical paradoxes including Gödel's Undecidability Theorem by developing Operator Logic and Quantum Operator Logic; first developed a quantitative harmonic oscillator-like model of the life cycle, and interactions, of civilizations; first showed how equations describing superorganisms also apply to civilizations. A recent book shows his theory applies successfully to the past 14 years of history and to *new* archaeological data on Andean and Mayan civilizations as well as Early Anatolian and Egyptian civilizations.

He first developed an axiomatic derivation of the forms of The Standard Model from geometry – space-time properties – The Extended Standard Model. It has a Dark Matter sector that approximates the ElectroWeak sector with Dark doublets and Dark gauge interactions. It also uses quantum coordinates to remove infinities that crop up in most interacting quantum field theories and additionally to remove the infinities that appear in the Big Bang and generate inflationary growth of the universe. The Extended Standard Model is expanded into The Extended SuperStandard Model presented in this volume andvolume 1.

Blaha has had a major impact on a succession of elementary particle theories: his Ph.D. thesis (1970), and papers, showed that quantum field theory calculations to all orders in ladder approximations could not give scaling deep inelastic electron-nucleon scattering. He later showed the eigenvalue equation for the fine structure constant α in Johnson-Baker-Willey QED had a zero at $\alpha = 1$ not $1/137$ by solving the Schwinger-Dyson equations to all orders in an approximation that agreed with exact results to 4th order in α thus ending interest in this theory. In 1979 at Prof. Ken Johnson's (MIT) suggestion he calculated the proton-neutron mass difference in the MIT bag model and found the result had the wrong sign reducing interest in the bag model. These results all appear in Physical Review papers. In the 2000's he repeatedly pointed out the shortcomings of SuperString theory and showed that The Standard Model's form could be derived from space-time geometry by an extension of Lorentz transformations to faster than light transformations. This deeper space-time basis greatly increases the possibility that it is part of THE fundamental theory.Recently, Blaha showed that the Weak interactions differed significantly from the Strong, electromagnetic and gravitation interactions in important respects while these interactions had similar features, and suggested that ElectroWeak theory, which is essentially a glued union of the Weak interactions and Electromagnetism, possibly modulo unknown Higgs particle features, be replaced by a unified theory of the other interactions combined with a stand-alone Weak interaction theory. Blaha also showed that, if Charmonium calculations are taken seriously, the Strong interaction coupling constant is only a factor of five larger than the electromagnetic coupling constant, and thus Strong interaction perturbation theory would make sense and yield physically meaningful results.

In graduate school (1965-71) he wrote substantial papers in elementary particles and group theory: The Inelastic E- P Structure Functions in a Gluon Model. Phys. Lett. B40:501-502,1972; Deep-Inelastic E-P Structure Functions In A Ladder Model With Spin 1/2 Nucleons, Phys.Rev. D3:510-523,1971; Continuum Contributions To The Pion Radius, Phys. Rev. 178:2167-2169,1969; Character Analysis of U(N) and SU(N), J. Math. Phys. 10, 2156 (1969); and The Calculation of the Irreducible Characters of the Symmetric Group in Terms of the Compound Characters, (Published as Blaha's Lemma in D. E. Knuth's book: *The Art of Computer Programming Vols. 1 – 4*).

In the early 1980's Blaha was also a pioneer in the development of UNIX for financial, scientific and Internet applications: benchmarked UNIX versions showing that block size was critical for UNIX performance, developing financial modeling software, starting database benchmarking comparison studies, developing Internet-like UNIX networking (1982) and developing a hybrid shell programming technique (1982) that was a precursor to the PERL programming language. He was also the manager of the AT&T ten-year future products development database. His work helped lead to commercial UNIX on computers such as Sun Micros, IBM AIX minis, and Apple computers.

In the 1980's he pioneered the development of PC Desktop Publishing on laser printers. and was nominated for three "Awards for Technical Excellence" in 1987 by PC Magazine for PC software products that he designed and developed.

Recently he has developed a theory of Megaverses – actual universes of which our universe is one – with quantum particle-like properties based on the Wheeler-DeWitt equation of Quantum Gravity. He has developed a theory of a baryonic force, which had been conjectured many years ago, and estimated the strength of the force based on discrepancies in measurements of the gravitational constant G. This force, operative in D-dimensinal space, can be used to escape from our universe in "uniships" which are the equivalent of the faster-than-light starships proposed in the author's earlier books. Thus travel to other universes, as well as to other stars is possible.

Blaha also considered the complexified Wheeler-DeWitt equation and showed that its limitation to real-valued coordinates and metrics generated a Cosmological Constant in the Einstein equations.

The author has also recently written a series of books on the serious problems of the United States and their solution as well as a book on the decline of Mankind that will follow from current social and genetic trends in Mankind.

In the past twelve years Dr. Blaha has written over 40 books on a wide range of topics. Some recent major works are: *From Asynchronous Logic to The Standard Model to Superflight to the Stars, All the Universe!, SuperCivilizations: Civilizations as Superorganisms, America's Future: an Islamic Surge, ISIS, al Qaeda, World Epidemics, Ukraine, Russia-China Pact, US Leadership Crisis,The Rises and Falls of Man – Destiny – 3000 AD: New Support for a Superorganism MACRO-THEORY of CIVILIZATIONS From CURRENT WORLD TRENDS and NEW Peruvian, Pre-Mayan, Mayan, Anatolian, and Early Egyptian Data, with a Projection to 3000 AD,* and *Mankind in Decline: Genetic Disasters, Human-Animal Hybrids, Overpopulation, Pollution, Global Warming, Food and Water Shortages, Desertification, Poverty, Rising Violence, Genocide, Epidemics, Wars, Leadership Failure.*

He has taught approximately 4,000 students in undergraduate, graduate, and postgraduate corporate education courses primarily in major universities, and large companies and government agencies.

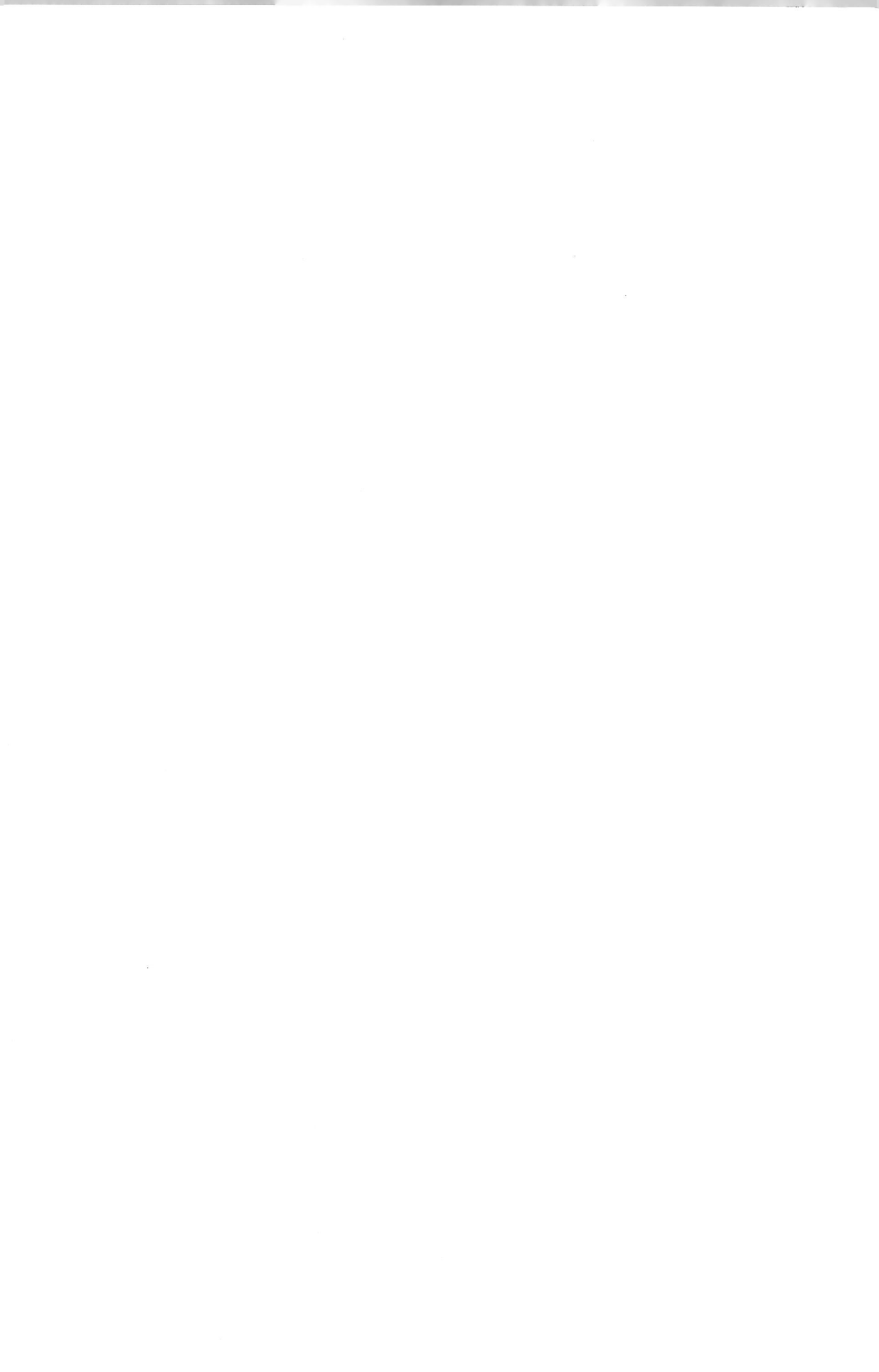